Unstuck

FREEING YOURSELF FROM THE GRIPS OF
YOUR SAFETY NET AND LIVING THE LIFE
OF PURPOSE YOU WERE MADE FOR

LORI SANDERS

LIFEWISE BOOKS

Unstuck

FREEING YOURSELF FROM THE GRIPS OF YOUR SAFETY NET AND LIVING THE LIFE OF PURPOSE YOU WERE MADE FOR

BY LORI SANDERS

Published by:

LIFEWISE BOOKS

PO BOX 1072
Pinehurst, TX 77362
LifeWiseBooks.com

To contact the author: LoriSanders.com

ISBN (Print): 978-1-952247-11-8
ISBN (Ebook): 978-1-952247-12-5

Dedication

To Rick and Guy, for your continual love, support, and encouragement. Thank you for helping me follow and live out my dream. I love you both, *all* the time!

Contents

Introduction

GOODBYE DREAM

I remember the exact moment I abandoned my dream. I was in college. Photography had been my passion ever since I received my first camera as a child. In high school, I learned about photography as an art form, not just a way to record family events. I immersed myself in learning all I could. After graduation, I was hired as a receptionist at a photography studio. I signed up for photography courses in college and continued taking photography-related jobs throughout my undergraduate years.

I worked as a clerk at a camera store, an event staff photographer, and earned a position as a photographer for the school newspaper. I even began getting photos published. I saw everything through a camera lens and dreamed of having my photos in *Rolling Stone* or *National Geographic* magazines; however, at some point, I told myself I would never make it. My dream seemed too big. So, without even giving myself a chance, I gave up.

WHAT NOW?

Without any plan or reasoning, I picked a major in art and design with an emphasis in interior design. I spent over a year struggling through numerous architecture and design courses, and nearly every project I turned in was a disaster. My grades reflected the fact that I didn't grasp the concepts; I received one B, three Cs, and one D. Whereas, I always excelled in my photography courses and got As.

I do remember one design assignment I enjoyed: a group project constructing a chair out of cardboard. We worked late into the night and created a chair our professors approved. This was the first time I can remember discovering my enjoyment of brainstorming and working as a team. Still, there was no denying that interior design was not my lane.

Even though I knew photography was my passion, what I was good at, and what I wanted to study, I was encouraged to take an interest inventory. Speech-language pathology appeared on the list of careers best suited for me. I had no idea what it was, but it sounded impressive and safe. So, I found a college offering that degree and moved forward.

I loved my courses, professors, and classmates. I thoroughly enjoyed studying and learning. After six years of undergrad and two years of graduate school, I finally graduated. I walked away with a master's degree in communication disorders, a bound master's thesis, a publication in an educational journal, and a mountain of student loan debt. A year later, I was working in a long-term care facility and making a considerable salary with a 401K, health insurance, and continuing-education reimbursement. I felt successful and secure. I felt I had made it.

While I had abandoned my dream of being a photographer, I kept it as a hobby and it fed my creative outlet for over twenty years, but I always wondered what I could have accomplished if only I had given myself a chance.

A NEW DREAM

Twenty years later, another dream emerged, and this time I didn't want to let it slip away. But what was I to do? How could I let go of the career I had studied so long for and the job that gave me a steady paycheck and insurance benefits? This job was my safety net, my security blanket. However, it was beginning to stifle the desires of my heart and soul.

This is my story about finding the courage to follow what I felt was not only a dream but a calling and what I discovered along the way.

START YOUR JOURNEY NOW

If you have abandoned a dream, gotten lost along the way, or reached a dead-end, I have written this book for you. I want to share my journey to give you hope that it's not too late to live out your dream. Right where you are, you can begin your journey toward living the life of purpose you have been dreaming of. This book is about embracing the dream stirring inside you, the one setting your heart and soul on fire and making you come alive.

I will share with you steps you can take to start your unique journey. Each step you take and each path you follow will shape and prepare you. At the end of each chapter, I've included a call to action with questions to get you thinking and steps for you to take, along with a prayer to help you take them. Get ready to be reacquainted with yourself as you follow the twists and turns and highs and lows of this incredible expedition.

You can find the strength and tools you
need to embrace and live the dream you
don't feel equipped for, that seems out
of reach, the one everyone thinks is crazy,
the one that is just too big—that dream.

My desire is for you to come alive and experience the feeling accomplishment brings even before you finish reading this book, but first you have to *move*. You have to take a step forward. Don't let fear take the wheel. Be bold, be brave, get unstuck, and start living your dream and fulfilling the purpose God has planned for you.

Chapter 1

BEING STUCK

"Sometimes it's not until you see your shackles that you see your dreams. The soul must first be caged before it can be set free."[1]

—Ken Ilgunas

WHEN THE LIGHT GOES OUT. . .

After twenty-two years as a speech-language pathologist, the light seemed to turn off, just like that. I was no longer interested in continuing my profession. I loved my coworkers who had become like family, but the work itself was no longer exciting to me.

Over the years, I had enjoyed the people I worked with and the students I treated. I had eagerly served on committees, taken leadership positions, studied, learned, and tried new things, but now, I was dragging myself to work each day, sitting alone at my computer writing reports, or preparing for meetings.

I had less interaction with my students because an assistant did most of the therapy. Working only part-time limited my interactions with my team, and the work was becoming monotonous. I walked into work and functioned most of the day on autopilot. My sense of purpose was diminishing, and I was growing very discontent.

It seemed I was living Groundhog Day. I didn't feel like I was growing, and nothing seemed to inspire me. I was simply getting my work done and collecting a paycheck. I realized I was complaining a lot to my coworkers and was no longer the supportive and upbeat professional I used to be.

I felt used up and burnt out, and I couldn't see a light at the end of the tunnel. As it turned out, I was not alone.

BURNOUT

Burnout has become so common it is listed in the *11th Revision of the International Classification of Diseases (ICD-11)* as an occupational phenomenon.[2]

Burnout is described by the *ICD-11 for Mortality and Morbidity Statistics* as "a syndrome conceptualized as resulting from chronic workplace stress that has not been successfully managed."[3] It is characterized by three dimensions referring to the context of the workplace:

- feelings of energy depletion or exhaustion
- increased mental distance from one's job, or feelings of negativism or cynicism related to one's job
- reduced professional efficacy[4]

I wasn't necessarily feeling exhausted, but I didn't feel I was contributing much to my profession. I felt utterly disconnected from what I had been doing for twenty-two years. I yearned for a change in my life.

HOW DID I END UP HERE?

How could the light go out on something I had spent so much time pursuing and at one time loved doing? Could it be because the career I chose was not something I longed to do but rather an option I picked off a list in an attempt to fulfill cultural expectations?

I was confused because I had enjoyed college. I enjoyed learning and acquiring the skills I needed in my field. I loved my internships and the experiences I gained. I loved writing and researching. As graduation day grew closer and I began applying for jobs, my professors encouraged me to continue my studies and get a PhD so I could teach, but after eight years of study, I was ready to get out and work. Looking back now, I think maybe they could see something in me I couldn't.

Still, I did not know what I wanted to do, so I decided to follow the money. Having a job with a sizable salary and benefits says, "It was worth it" and "I am successful." It was confirmation that I made the right choice. However, after only two years as a professional, there were significant changes in the health-care industry, resulting in downsizing and even companies dissolving. At one point, some of my coworkers weren't even getting paychecks.

I began rethinking the security of my job and moved into what seemed the safest arena—public schools. I took a massive pay cut, but it was safe. While I can't say, even after twenty-two years, I was raking in the dough, my paycheck had allowed for a comfortable lifestyle when combined with my husband's salary. Still, I wondered, *What if I had done what I really wanted to do?*

Ken Ilgunas talks about his experience of getting stuck in his book *Walden on Wheels*. He says, "I went to high school because I was forced to; I went to college because I was supposed to; and now I'd enter the career world because I was financially obligated to."[5]

He got stuck by following the expectations of his parents and his culture. I got stuck because I was too scared to jump off the path of security. Ilgunas later said, "Freedom was simply being able to entertain the prospect of changing your circumstances."[6]

Tim Mannin talks about how as children we learn to dream, and as we grow up, those dreams are squelched because we are expected to have responsible careers and abandon our dreams to follow "prescribed action steps."[7]

I had followed those prescribed action steps. I don't remember anyone telling me I had to go to college. It was just what everyone I knew did. You followed the plan: graduate from high school, go to college, pick a major, graduate, and get a job.

I don't remember ever talking to anyone about my skills or dreams or what options were available. I just signed up for required courses, and of course, photography courses. I was wandering aimlessly to some foreign destination because I was too fearful of following the path I dreamed of traveling.

My heart said, "Go!" and my head
said, "Is that really a good idea?"

Looking back, I can see that getting stuck was a gradual process. What led me there was the loss of the things that I loved best about all the jobs I had. Over time, I recognized the common factors. Determining what they were helped me move forward. I only started discovering those as I got closer to making the big decision to get unstuck.

You are reading this book, so I think it is safe to say that you are at some level of being stuck and have stirrings inside for something more. I want you to know, it is possible to break free from the safety net that provides comfort yet keeps you from living a life of purpose and fulfillment. You can begin, right now, to use your God-given gifts and talents to breathe life into your dream and become the person you were meant to be.

CALL TO ACTION

Write down what is making you feel stuck.

Make a list of elements about your current and previous work that energize you and those that deplete you.

What would you like to change about your current situation?

Prayer

Dear Lord,

I am thankful for the opportunities I have had
and the people who have taught and mentored
me. I am grateful for the journey that has led
me where I am today. However, the light in me
has faded, and I feel a longing for something
different in my life. I feel a calling to change.
Please help me to determine when and where I
need to move.

Amen.

Chapter 2

THE STIRRINGS INSIDE

"We're all yearning for a wedge of sky, aren't we? I suspect God plants these yearnings in us so we'll at least try and change the course of things. We must try, that's all."

—Sue Monk Kidd[1]

During this time of being stuck, something started stirring inside me: the desire to write. Like photography, writing was also something I had discovered in high school. I had signed up for marine biology, and after day one, studying the chemistry of water and not whales and dolphins, I immediately requested a change.

A creative writing class was available. I took it and loved it. Writing allowed me a way to let go of all the thoughts in my head, to let my imagination run wild, create new worlds, and find ways to describe what I saw and felt.

After high school, I continued to write, mostly poems for myself and others close to me, but that was about it. I never pursued writing publicly. Again, after some reflection, I recalled that many of the classes I enjoyed in college involved writing, all kinds of writing—essays, speeches, and research.

Over twenty years later, surviving the devastation of Hurricane Harvey led me to submit an article and a poem about my experience. I had hesitations and doubts about submitting my work, but something was pushing me. I was afraid of being rejected, but eventually, I mustered up the courage and submitted them. To my surprise, they both were accepted and published. My writing bug had been awakened and was hungry!

This was the reassurance I needed to get moving. There is a quote from Paulo Coelho's book *The Alchemist* that says, "And when you want something, all the universe conspires in helping you to achieve it."[2] This seemed to be the case because I kept encountering more and more about writing. Something would pop up on social media, I would get a random email, I would meet someone, or hear about something on a podcast. Everywhere I looked, there was something inviting me to write.

It wasn't easy to ignore the stirrings getting louder and louder. I couldn't ignore my desire to write and connect with people about issues other than speech and language disorders. I really wanted to quit my job. Quitting would allow me to pursue writing and photography and be at home to do more for my family. But why would I do that when my job provided me a paycheck and benefits? Why would I leave my safety net? While the work wasn't inspiring me, it was easy, and yes, it was safe.

I began writing on the side and started a new blog and an Instagram account where I posted my photos. I could continue to work and keep writing articles, right? I could, however, I was becoming increasingly uncomfortable and began to wrestle more and more with what I should do.

A SHORT FILM AND EMILY P. FREEMAN

Sitting in my office eating lunch at my desk, I happened upon a short, animated film called *Alike*[3] It is the story of a father and son whose color and creativity are literally drained from their bodies as they perform the monotonous tasks related to work and school.

The characters in the film resonated with me. I felt as if the color was draining out of me. Watching the color drain out of the child made me think of my own son. I did not want to push these cultural expectations on him. I didn't want his creativity to be squelched and have him end up burnt out. I wanted us to live in color.

> At this point, the stirrings were becoming persistent. I couldn't stop dreaming about writing and being free from the constraints of my job.

The stirrings were making me crazy until I changed my perspective with the help of author Emily P. Freeman. I had heard about Emily on a podcast. I looked her up and began to listen to her podcast, *The Next Right Thing*. I came across one episode called "Quit Something."[4] The title certainly piqued my interest because I was considering quitting something myself.

As I drove down the highway, I listened in awe as I heard Emily say, "There's something strong I can't shake, something I think the Lord is drawing me to. 'It's time to write,' I hear on the level of my soul. I'm excited and also terrified. Yellow is dancing around in my head. Writing is yellow; the things that make us come alive always are."[5]

I had to pull over, rewind, and replay. Emily had put my thoughts and feelings into words. There was a yearning in the depths of my soul to write, creating waves of excitement and waves of terror as I thought about leaving my safety net. I imagined yellow rays of life-giving energy shining on my face, wrapping me in a warm embrace, making me feel tranquil and energized at the same time.

This was how I felt when I wrote. I thought maybe I understood what Emily meant by "yellow." I had to do something. I was ready for a change, but after so long in the same career, I didn't know where to start, how to start, or even why to start.

It was a big decision and a big move, so I prayed for guidance. I was excited thinking about writing and photography. Quitting my job would allow me to be creative, interact more with my writing groups, have a flexible schedule, work from home, and take better care of myself and my family.

I prayed for God to send me signs to know if I was making the right decision, and it started raining signs. One sign in particular that kept showing up—literally on signs—was a quote attributed to Mother Teresa: "If you want to change the world, go home and love your family."[6]

Not long after that, I heard the song "Reason" on the radio. I felt as if God were sending me a musical message, another confirmation. I sat in the parking lot, downloaded the song, and read over the lyrics. These words spoke to me: "He put that hunger in your heart. He put that fire in your soul. When you feel like giving up, when you feel like giving in, His love is the reason, to keep on believing."[7]

Okay, I thought. *This is from God.* It has to be. I decided it was time to follow the signs.

CALL TO ACTION

Watch the short film *Alike.* www.alike.es

Describe in detail what you do or imagine doing that makes you feel alive and fills you with color. Try not to spend too much time thinking about it. Just let the words flow.

What activities/websites/books are you drawn to?

Make a list of groups you would be interested in joining.

If location and money were not a concern, what would you want to do?

Prayer

Dear Lord,

I pray for clarity. Help me to understand this yearning and desire you have given me. Send me signs of confirmation so I can faithfully take steps forward.

Amen.

Chapter 3

WHAT'S HOLDING YOU BACK?

"When you've got a vision, you don't have time to wait around for your fears to vanish before you start moving."[1]

—Jessica Honegger

CONQUERING FEAR

Over the years, I have watched my husband take on many challenges with ease. He is a doer. He doesn't hesitate or second-guess himself. The task might not be easy, but his decision to start something new is. I am quite the opposite, a dreamer, with my head in the clouds. I've been that way all my life. I would dream but never move forward. It was far easier to just imagine doing something amazing.

I often wonder what makes the doers move and the dreamers stand still. It's as if one person confidently runs into the waves and the other person stands on the shore, wanting to share in the excitement but bound to the sand. Before I began writing this book, I was the one standing on the shore, tethered by fear.

I was letting fear push me around like a playground bully. My doubts began to pile up, and the "what ifs" took over.

I thought, *What if I make the wrong decision? What if I quit my job and end up regretting it? What if I fail, let everyone down, and look like a fool? What if? What if? What if?* In her book, *Love Lives Here*, Maria Goff says, "Fear is never content on the fringes; it always demands center stage."[2] I had pulled back the curtains, more than once, and given fear the starring role.

I was fearful of change. While my job wasn't satisfying my need to create, it was easy and comfortable. I could show up and follow the well-established routine until the end of the day. Starting a career in writing would force me into a world I knew almost nothing about. I didn't know what I was doing besides putting words on paper. I feared people would consider me unqualified because I didn't have any formal training and wasn't well-read and, therefore, would not want to read what I had written.

I feared failure. What if I never published anything again? What if I spent thousands of dollars and never made a dime? What if I failed, and it was all for nothing? As much as I feared failure, I also feared success. I feared people reading the pages, seeing my vulnerability. I feared I was too old. I was intimidated by the young, emerging writers who seemed to be so much more knowledgeable and connected with large social media followings.

However, what I feared most was, what if I hadn't really heard God calling me to write? What if this whole writing dream was just that, a dream? Something I had concocted as part of a midlife crisis? I also feared by following my dream, I was being selfish—pursuing a dream and letting my husband foot the bill.

After a lot of pondering and thoughtful prayer, I made up my mind and got my husband's blessing. Still second-guessing my decision and all the signs telling it was time for change, I returned to the cycle of indecision fueled by fear, and there I sat scared to turn in my resignation letter and seal the deal.

I found more encouragement from Emily P. Freeman. She writes, "If God has something to tell you, and you continu̶ ᴖ place yourself before him, he won't let you miss̶ ᴵᴛ. As you take your next right step today, trust ᴛhat God won't let you miss your own future."[3]

MAKING SENSE OF GOD'S PLAN

It was starting to make sense, but I needed more clarity. I dug a little deeper and tried to make sense of the hunger in my heart and fire in my soul—as described by the song—and tried to make sure that God put it there.

I picked up my Bible and noted these truths:

God has plans for me. Plans to prosper me and not to harm me, plans to give me a hope and a future (Jeremiah 29:11).

God will instruct me and teach me the way (Psalm 32:8).

When I have trust and faith, God will make my paths straight. (Proverbs 3:5–6).

He will fulfill his purpose for me (Philippians 1:6).

He won't abandon me (Joshua 1:9).

These verses helped me take the emphasis off me and my plan, and how I thought it should play out, and focus on God and his plan. I came to the conclusion that I didn't need to aspire to have writing as a profession but as a mission. I sealed the letter of resignation and sent it in.

GETTING IN THE DEEP END

After several swimming lessons, my son was able to cross over the ropes into the deep end. He would stand on the edge of the pool, boldly jump in, sink down, and bubble back up to the surface, wearing expressions of excitement, uncertainty, and a little bit of fear.

After he caught his breath, he would climb out and jump in again. Each time, he became more confident. As swimming became more natural, uncertainty and fear faded, but the excitement continued.

Maybe you have been avoiding crossing over to the deep end, favoring the shallow end where your feet can touch the bottom. I think we all fear venturing into the deep end where we can't touch or even see the bottom. It's safe over in the shallow end. There, we can't get in over our heads.

> If you are feeling called to do something new and different, at some point, you need to jump in and experience the uncertainty and fear along with the excitement as you live out God's purpose in your life.

It's so easy to stay in your safe place, especially when it seems too hard and the obstacles seem too big. When doubt and discouragement steal your momentum, it's easy to want to stay or return to what you know. I can tell you even as I write this book, when it gets hard, I doubt my decision and consider giving up. That is when I return to those Bible verses and get my second, third, fourth, or fifth wind.

I heard a story of conquistadors arriving in a new land. They must have been excited and relieved to finally reach their destination after months at sea; however, they must have also been intimidated not knowing what to expect. As fear and doubt set in, it may have seemed easier to get back on the ships and sail home, rather than learning to live in uncharted territory full of uncertainly. Eventually, the captain gave orders to burn the ships, keeping anyone from abandoning the mission and returning to the safety of the homeland.

God has given us each dreams and passions to explore, requiring patience, perseverance, and faith. Buckle up and be willing to let God transform you. Be brave, embrace change, and get ready to burn the ships.

Author Anne Lamott says, "Life is going by very quickly, and if you're not careful, you're gonna be eighty years old and have spent your life wishing that you'd have gotten your work done."[4]

Don't make your only failure, not trying.

CALL TO ACTION

Make a list of everything you feel is holding you back.

What are your fears?

Write down at least one way you can overcome your fears and move forward.

Prayer

Dear Lord,

I have a desire growing inside of my heart, and I really feel you calling me to move. Help me exchange my fear for courage, knowing you will guide me, instruct me, and see me through this journey until the end.

Amen.

Chapter 4

USE WHAT YOU'VE GOT

"Your talent is God's gift to you. What you do with it is
your gift back to God."

—Leo Buscaglia[1]

The apostle Paul urges us to live a life worthy of the
calling we have received, saying each one of us has
a special gift that God has generously given to us
(Ephesians 4:7).

Unlocking your gifts and talents to pursue your purpose
sounds complicated and can be overwhelming to think
about. Many of us have more than an inkling of what
we are good at, but we let fear keep us from using it to
its full potential.

As I mentioned earlier, for two decades, photography
was my passion. I loved everything about it and believe

it was a special gift. I just wasn't ever brave enough to let it shine entirely, and for some reason, my passion faded. I tried to force myself to feel the desire again by purchasing a new camera. I thought it would inspire me, but it never did. My pretty red camera sat gathering dust.

Even though photography was never my career, it was a huge part of my identity. The awards and publications I had told me I was accomplished, and my work had value. Still, the desire was gone, and I had to be willing to let it go.

> I had to loosen my grip, so I could accept something different.

If you are like me and don't follow up with one dream, I think God will stir up another one. While I was mourning the doused desire for photography, writing was lighting my soul on fire. It was my new passion. But was it a spiritual gift, was it a calling? I still didn't know for sure, but it was time to find out.

I had an opportunity to write full time and was ready to start stepping out to determine if writing was a gift. If it was, I was going to write and then be prepared to let it go if God gave me a new dream, a new passion, a new purpose.

Before I realized how much I loved writing, I started a blog called *Permission to Dream, Heart and Soul*. On Sunday, June 13, 2010, I published my first blog post showcasing one of my photographs and a quote: "The day came when the risk to remain tight in a bud was more painful than the risk it took to blossom"[2]

I followed up with my own words: "For me, that time has come. So I take the risk to blossom, to begin living my dreams. I am tossing out my security blanket and stepping out of my comfort zone. It's a bit frightening but exhilarating at the same time. I have to answer the call to create. Has your day come?"

I created the blog mainly to display my photography and connect with other artists. I never considered that I was writing. Perhaps God was using that dream to prepare me for the journey I'm on now.

During that time, I also opened an art gallery. There I continued to write for my blog and work on my photography. I also developed a photography e-course, hosted a photography contest, and connected with artists online and in my community. I learned about running a business.

Although I enjoyed this venture, I wasn't enjoying the lack of customers. I grew bored with the quiet, and after six months, I returned to work at my old job as a speech-language pathologist. It was a fabulous season I recall fondly and will never regret. I discovered I may not be cut out to own or run a store, but I loved creating, teaching, researching, and writing. Looking back, these were the same aspects I enjoyed in my years as a speech-language pathologist. I think it is what kept me going so long. Only now, I wasn't doing any of that.

When I look back over the years, I discovered I was happiest and most productive when I was working as a team, planning a project, learning something new, or doing something creative. As I realized this, I began to look for something that allowed me to do all of these things.

WHEN THE GOING GETS TOUGH

Don't get discouraged if you can't see how your past experiences can help develop your future and serve your calling. Just having the hunger burning inside you is a start. Let God begin to mold you. He will magnify in you what you think is small and insignificant. He will give you all the things you need to do his work (2 Corinthians 9:8).

One of my favorite fictional examples of God calling a person, equipping him, and allowing him to live his dream comes from an unlikely source. There is a movie from 2007 called *Evan Almighty*.[3] In this comedy, God calls a newly appointed congressman to build an ark in the middle of suburbia. He gives him all the tools he needs, literally delivering them in a box on his doorstep.

Evan ignores the call, which seems ridiculous and impossible. When he finally gives in, God brings everything together, helping him accomplish the mission. Evan's dream was to change the world, and with God's direction, he did. His dream just wasn't delivered in packaging he recognized.

When your dream seems impossible and you feel like you are far from your target, consider each step in your journey one point, more like dot-to-dot than a bull's-eye. We can only see each dot, but God can see the big picture. To us, each dot may seem insignificant, but when you combine them, they make sense and create something amazing.

Jennie Allen writes, "The Spirit of God has dreams for you. And He has given you an abundance of gifts, resources, people and vision to accomplish *His* dreams for you. If you do not feel that way yet, you will."[4]

We must keep moving toward the finish line, that last dot, using everything God has given us. Continue putting one foot in front of the other, even when it gets hard. We can lean on God, take that cup of water he is offering, and be confident he will be there at the finish line waiting for us.

"Let us run with perseverance the race marked out for us, fixing our eyes on Jesus, the pioneer and perfecter of faith" (Hebrews 12:1-2).

CALL TO ACTION

Complete the Personality Inventory at the end of this book.

Write down three things that you enjoy talking about or doing.

Is there something that people seem to always ask you to do, for example, bake, style, design, listen, or give advice?

What do you not like doing?

Prayer

Dear Lord,

Please help me see more clearly the gifts and talents you have given me and how I can use those to feed the yearnings in my soul. Guide me to the tools, resources, and people who can help me live out the plan you have for me.

Amen.

Chapter 5

WHAT DRIVES YOU?

"Being driven is not the same as being passionate.
Passion is a love for the journey. Drive is a need
to reach the destination."

—Simon Sinek[1]

NOT KNOWING WHY

Several years ago, there was a catchphrase going around that said, "Know your why." The school district where I worked adopted it as a theme one year, and we were asked to consider our why. At that time, I was in the early stages of burnout, and the only answer I could come up with was "a paycheck."

Sadly, that was my why. It was the main reason I woke up every morning and went to work. However, looking back, I can say for most of my life, I have done things based on some pretty weak reasons, including it sounded fun, it was safe, and it was expected. Many times, the purpose was based on the outcome and nothing more.

This time felt different because I actually felt something bigger calling me to write. I felt God was calling me, but still, my why wasn't completely clear. Initially, I figured I should write a children's book since I had a background in child language development and had worked with children for the last twenty years. I thought I could somehow incorporate what I had learned. I felt it would justify me quitting my job and not feel like I had wasted all my college and professional years.

I wrote pages and pages of ideas and tried to come up with a story, but it never came to me. What did come to me was this book, this story. Still, it was not until I was several thousand words into it that I came upon a Bible verse, helping me honestly answer the question of why.

1 Peter 4:10 says, "Each of you should use whatever gift you have received to serve others, as faithful stewards of God's grace in its various forms."

Not long after that, I came across other verses that all pointed to the reason why.

Colossians 3:23 that says, "Whatever you do, work at it with all your heart, as working for the Lord, not for human masters."

David Ramos, the author of *What the Bible Says About Purpose*, points to Exodus 9:16 and explains, "Our primary calling in Scripture as humans is to glorify God. How that unfolds in our lives through our unique talents, gifts, and circumstances can end up looking a million different ways. But the end goal never changes. We are here for God's glory."[2]

In the book, *Ripple Effects,* Pam Tebow writes, "We face an ongoing battle for the right to rule our lives, but we will miss out on the opportunities, blessings, and positive influence when we run our own lives or choose any other master but the Lord."[3]

I sensed I had uncovered the final piece to the puzzle. I had a desire, a dream to write, I had been given a gift and an opportunity. God was joining me with people and resources to use my words to honor him and serve others. When I began to focus on this alignment, more doors began to open, and everything began to fall into place.

I believe knowing why gives you clarity and helps you create a goal. I think it gives you direction and keeps you in your lane. It motivates you to keep moving forward.

I found a great example of this by comedian Michael Jr. During a stand-up comic routine, he took a break to talk to a music director in the audience. He asked the man to sing a couple bars of "Amazing Grace." The man sang a delightful melody, and the audience clapped. Then Michael Jr. asked him to sing the version he would sing as if his uncle just got out of jail or he was shot in the back as a kid.

The man belted out a version that literally moved people right out of their seats. He sang with feeling and emotion because this time, he knew *why* he was singing. He was told both what to do and why to do it. Michael Jr. explains that *what* he does is comedy and why he does it is to inspire people to walk in purpose. He states that when you know your why your what becomes clear and more impactful.[4]

When you know your purpose and begin to walk in it, people will be drawn in wanting what you are offering because it moves them out of their seats.

Author Simon Sinek's website defines the why as "the purpose, cause or belief that drives every one of us," and he believes that knowing why will "guide you toward fulfillment in your work and life."[5]

If God was calling me to write, then my ultimate reason to move forward would be to honor him and serve others with the talents that he gave to me. This knowledge was going to keep me grounded. Knowing that I was working *for* God and *with* God was going to bring the purpose and fulfillment I desired.

Now I fully understood my primary purpose but still needed to figure out my secondary purpose.

In an interview with Rachel Hollis, Ken Coleman advises answering these three questions when trying to gain clarity about your purpose and to get your brain and heart to connect:

1. Who do I want to help?

2. What problem do I want to solve?

3. What solution do I want to provide?[6]

After taking some time to ponder these questions, I came up with my answers. I wanted to help anyone who was stuck like me, anyone who had settled into a safe place, letting fear stand in the way of freedom. I wanted to give them hope and let them know it's not too late and their dream is not too big. I wanted to show them the way to get unstuck and encourage them to take the first step to move toward their calling.

CALL TO ACTION

Get inspired by watching the video by Michael Jr. YouYube.com/watch?v=1ytFB8TrkTo.

Write down your primary why.

Answer the three questions posed by Ken Coleman:

1. Who do I want to help?

2. What problem do I want to solve?

3. What solution do I want to provide?

What opportunities are there in your own community to use your skills and talents?

Prayer

Dear Lord,

Help me to keep you first and make you the purpose of living out the dream you put in my heart. Guide me to use my gifts and talents to honor you, and lead me to those I can serve.

Amen.

Chapter 6

CLEARING SPACE AND TIME

"Clutter is not just the stuff on your floor
—it's anything that stands between you and
the life you want to be living."

—Peter Walsh[1]

GETTING STARTED

Now that you have a better understanding of what you want to do and why you want to do it, I want you to consider one more thing before you get moving: space. Before you start to establish a foundation, you have to clear space. As I began my journey to become a writer, I had to clear a physical space to write without distractions, and I had to make mental space to keep me focused on why I wanted to write and what I had to say.

I thought of the acronym THINK, which I had seen floating around the internet for years. I'm not sure who coined it. It stands for true, helpful, inspiring, necessary, and kind. Its purpose is to make you think before you speak, not to say anything unless it is true, helpful, inspiring, necessary, or kind. It's a great way to keep yourself from wasting your words or saying anything that might embarrass you or hurt others.

I thought it would be helpful to utilize the acronym to help clear space as well. I would not fill my mind or space with negative clutter, only using thoughts and items that were true, helpful, inspiring, necessary, and kind. It's a dynamic process, one that I have to continually monitor.

Test prep coach, Erika Oppenheimer, says, "Having a clear mind and a clear space allows you to think and act with purpose,"[2] and professional organizer, Barbara Hemphill, believes, "Clutter is simply postposed decisions."[3] I agree and have seen the effects firsthand. Make the decision to clear the clutter before you create.

BEGIN WITH A MANTRA

Look anywhere, and you will find coffee cups, clothing, and home decor with inspirational quotes and Bible verses. Although the intentions are well-meaning, I have come to see that an abundance of messages can be overwhelming and quickly lose their value. A quote or verse that speaks to you can soon become part of the scenery you pass each day without notice.

I encourage you to choose one or two quotes or verses that inspire you as you start your journey. There is no need to buy a sweatshirt or large sign for your living room. Try a sticky note on the bathroom mirror or in your workspace. You might even want to rewrite it each day to keep you motivated. Let this become your daily mantra.

CREATE A VISION

Seeing is believing. Close your eyes and picture yourself doing the thing you are dreaming of doing. Where are you? What are you wearing? Who is with you? You can achieve it, but there is work to be done. The goal is to live the dream but not live in a dream world. Your vision will help you stay focused when the work gets hard, and it *will* get hard. Imagine a new mother holding her baby. The work that it takes to get the baby in her arms is exhausting and painful, but the vision keeps her focused. Even after sleepless nights and endless diaper changes, women keep having babies. They know the hard work and pain that comes with having a baby, but the vision and the feeling of hearts overflowing with love and joy make it worth it.

My husband had a vision for our ranch. Before we even bought cows, we had to clear the land, put up fences to create pastures, create shelters, plant grass, and buy feed and other supplies. Once established, there was still work to do to keep the vision alive. Maintenance is required despite our unpredictable Texas weather.

My husband endures torn clothes and skin from barbed wire, equipment breaking, fences falling, stubborn animals, and the occasional days when he walks back in socks because his boots got stuck in the mud. Interestingly enough, on the days when the weather is at its worst, or the work has been extra difficult, he comes home with a smile on his face, feeling a sense of accomplishment in living out his vision.

One way to keep your vision alive is to create a vision board. You can use a cork board or just a piece of paper. Write down relevant words and add pictures, photos, or objects to inspire and motivate you. Keep it in your work area or where you can see it daily.

CLEAR A SPACE FOR WORK

I needed a home office to set up my writing space. I created one in a tiny spare bedroom upstairs, which also doubles as my closet. As I began to transform it, I tried to make it both comfortable and functional. I gathered what I needed and worked to keep the rest out of sight.

I hung curtains to separate my clothes from the desk, removed numerous decorations that were not needed, and discovered when I write I have to remove everything on my desk except for a notepad and a pen. I can't keep bills or to-do lists on it because it draws my attention away from what I am creating.

Determine where you need to work and what tools or supplies you need. You might need space in your kitchen, garden, or garage. You might need to inquire about renting a studio space. Resist the urge to gather more than you need to start.

> I encourage you to take time to grow into your dream and invest gradually as it begins to blossom.

CLEAR TIME FOR STILLNESS

Remember when you used to get a busy signal when you called someone and they were on the phone? For those of you who don't know about this, it was a repetitive, beeping sound. When you heard it, you would hang up and try calling back later.

In today's world, busyness has become a badge of honor. "I'm so busy" has become the filler replacing, "I'm fine," when someone asks how we are doing. We fill our days with distractions leaving little or no time to be still and quiet, preventing us from talking to or hearing from God. The creator of all the universe wants to speak to us, and he is getting a busy signal.

Carve out some daily time for you and God. He has great things to share with you. Quiet time also allows you to free your mind of the continual bombardment of information and just be. It allows you time to rest, reflect, restore, and recharge. You might be surprised how clear your thoughts become when you incorporate this practice into your day.

As you make progress and your vision becomes apparent, it will be easier to declutter knowing what you need and do not need.

CALL TO ACTION

Write down two verses or quotes that are meaningful to you and will help you move closer to fulfilling your dream.

Gather some art supplies and begin creating your vision board. Let your imagination run free; don't put limits on your dream.

Designate a space for working and begin to clear the clutter. Start by merely throwing out trash and then eliminating items not associated with your vision. If you are not ready to throw them out or donate them, simply pack them away in a box and place them out of sight.

Designate a space for stillness. Put a copy of your mantra there. Add a few items that make you feel relaxed. Avoid using any electronics. Use this time for prayer and reflection. You might want to keep a notepad and pen handy for ideas that pop into your head.

Prayer

Dear Lord,

Help me to clear the clutter from my mind and my workspace so I can focus on the work you want me to do. Draw me closer to you and help me eliminate items that do not serve in carrying out my purpose.

Amen.

Chapter 7

CREATING A PATH

"When Jesus invites us on an adventure, He shapes
who we become with what happens along the way."

—Bob Goff[1]

THE MISSION

When traveling, you first have to decide on a
destination and then a plan on how to get there. When
I got my first car, a paper map was the only option to
plan my route. Current technology gives us details like
how long it will take and if there is a toll road that will
require payment, and when there is a closure, it gives
us options to get around it. While you won't have the
luxury of a GPS to guide your mission, it is helpful to
have a plan mapped out to guide you.

Until I began this journey, I never considered a plan and sometimes never even set a destination or goal. I just held on to a vague idea and spent a lot of time just wandering here and there. As you set out on your journey, a mission statement is a great way to keep you from wandering. Your mission statement will include what (your vision), how (your path), and why (your reason). Here are some examples I gathered after viewing several company websites.

TED[2]

What: "Our mission: Spread Ideas."

How: Providing a "clearinghouse of free knowledge from the world's most inspired thinkers."

Why: "We believe passionately in the power of ideas to change attitudes, lives and, ultimately, the world."

MAKE A WISH FOUNDATION[3]

What: "Together, we create life-changing wishes for children with critical illnesses."

How and Why: "We grant the wishes of children with life-threatening medical conditions to enrich human experience with hope, strength, and joy."

What: "Creating a culture of warmth and belonging, where everyone is welcome."

How and Why: "To inspire and nurture the human spirit, one person, one cup and one neighborhood at a time."

Look back over your notes from the previous chapters and consider what, how, and why. Use the space at the end of this chapter to write your mission statement. This statement is not set in stone. It is a dynamic plan that will grow and change as you do. One thing you can expect on this journey is change. There will be challenges, obstacles, detours, and sometimes you will take the scenic route instead of the fast track. Many different roads can lead to the same destinations, and the fastest one is not always the easiest one.

The first time I followed a dream and opened the art gallery, I didn't have many responsibilities. It was just my husband and me. I knew about art, and he knew about business. This time it wasn't as easy. We had a child and many more responsibilities. I couldn't just jump in.

While I was still working as a speech-language pathologist, I began aiming toward the goal of quitting my job to write. I put my entire paycheck into savings, started a new blog, and started submitting articles. I listened to podcasts and joined a writers group called hope*writers. They provide online courses, a library of resources, and a social media community to ask questions, share writing, and make connections. A member of hope*writers invited me to her local mastermind group, which eventually provided the connections and inspiration I needed to jump-start this writing journey.

START SMALL

Initially, I had no idea where to start. I thought maybe I needed a degree or expert training to begin writing professionally. However, as I started learning more about the craft and the business of writing and meeting other writers, I discovered I didn't need a degree to write. I could just start where I was and grow over time.

Ken Coleman offers the advice, "Start small, grow slow."[5] Sometimes I have to pull back the reins when my dreaming mind goes into overdrive. I have to say no to some opportunities and remind myself to take one step at a time, because each time I have tried to go big and fast, I ended up overspending time and money and becoming overwhelmed.

Don't get in line for the buffet, where you try everything and overload your plate. You'll end up stuffing yourself and feeling miserable. Pace yourself and enjoy each step of this journey. Build your product or craft, build your confidence, and learn from others.

> Make a move forward one step at a time, gather information, try something small. This is how you can mold your dream and let it begin to take shape.

Here are five ways to start small:

1. Make relationships.

Look for a group that shares your interest. The easiest way is through social media. Connecting with people on social media will likely lead to you a local group where you can meet with people in person and not only make connections but build relationships. You can also join or create a mastermind group. This is a group of peers that meet up to brainstorm or solve problems by giving one another advice and support.

The group I joined has a monthly meeting with a speaker and time for networking. It has allowed me to meet women who have different careers and are in different seasons of life but are all in various stages of the writing process. It was there I was able to connect with several women who have guided me on this journey and helped me achieve what I never believed I could.

2. Attend a workshop or conference.

Technology has allowed this to be a possibility no matter where you live. Many of the conferences I wanted to attend last year required a flight and several nights in a hotel, which was not ideal for me. Luckily, recordings from those conferences were available online for only a portion of the cost.

Two websites I love to learn from are creativelive.com and masterclass.com. Each has online courses taught by masters in several fields, allowing you to go at your own pace. You can watch in segments during your lunch break or after the kids go to bed.

3. Ask an expert.

Begin looking for people who share your interests or are already doing what you would like to do. When I have reached out to people asking for advice, I have always been pleasantly surprised how willing they were to help. When I worked as a speech-language pathologist, if I had a question about something, I would find out who the expert was in that area and email them. I can only think of one time when I didn't get a response.

I was amazed that the "celebrities" in my field were emailing me directly with answers to my questions and generously giving me advice and resources. Social media now makes this easier than ever.

4. Volunteer/offer a free service.

Look for opportunities to volunteer and share your talent. If you love animals and want to care for them, you can volunteer at the local animal shelter. If cooking is your thing, volunteer at a soup kitchen or homeless shelter. If you love to plan parties, volunteer to plan a birthday party or baby shower for a friend. Volunteering or providing a free service will give you some clarity about your vision and others' interest in it without much risk; plus, it's a great way to gather some testimonials.

5. Utilize social media.

In addition to being a great way to make connections, social media is also an excellent avenue to advertise and generate a conversation. I was listening to Brian Dixon, author of *Start with Your People*, being interviewed by Annie F. Downs on an episode of her podcast *This Sounds Fun*[6] He recommended a simple approach to starting small. He suggested asking a question regarding what you want to do on your personal social media page. See who responds, and then start a one-on-one conversation to gather specific information.

BUSINESSES THAT GREW FROM SMALL STARTS

Gemma of Champagne Cakery moved to my small town, not knowing a soul. She started baking at home and advertising her baked goods on social media. As her business grew, Gemma was able to access a professional kitchen and offer her products at a local coffee shop. Soon, orders were so numerous she had a waiting list for her delicious desserts. Starting small, she was able to determine there was enough interest in her product to open her own bakery.

Mark and Melanie of Javaman Coffee opened a small coffee shop in a suburban neighborhood. As their business grew, they were able to quit their jobs in professional sports and education to become full-time business owners. They started with coffee and pastries and eventually expanded their menu to breakfast and lunch items.

As their business continued to grow, they increased the size of the building and opened new locations in local grocery stores. After ten years of hard work, the original site has now become Javaman Coffee *and* Bistro.

Julie of The Bull Shack Coffee and Smoothies quit her job in the insurance industry to open a coffee and smoothie shop. This allowed her to work alongside her son and provide him an opportunity to continue his life skills. Initially, they opened a small shop in a location with other vendors. As they gained patrons and their business grew, they were able to build a stand-alone location.

WHAT HAPPENED NEXT

As I started on my path, I was amazed how doors were opening, and people and resources began pouring into my life. I was learning so much about myself, and my confidence was growing a little at a time.

> It was as if God was waiting for me
> to make a move. As I started to write,
> my path came more into focus.

Initially, my goal was to simply help one person. However, with some encouragement, my mission grew larger. I didn't want *anyone* to miss out on their dreams. If this project/dream/vision/mission is God's will, the possibilities are endless because my partner can do anything!

My hope is for you to take steps forward on your path, cultivating the life you are meant to live. Expect to learn things about yourself that you never knew. Your confidence will grow, as will your relationship with God, as you fulfill your purpose.

CALL TO ACTION

Put your what, how, and why together to complete your mission statement.

List names of people or groups you would like to connect with. Make a plan to contact at least one person or group within one week.

List two ways you can offer your skills.

Find a conference or online class you can attend to learn something new.

Ask a question on social media to generate a conversation about what you would like to do.

Prayer

Dear Lord,

Guide me to take each step in this path toward you. Lead me to the right people and places that can help me reach my destination. Keep me humble and keep me from rushing ahead of you.

Amen.

Chapter 8

OVERCOMING OBSTACLES

"Nothing that's worthwhile is ever easy. Remember that."
—Nicholas Sparks[1]

According to findmymarathon.com, 724 marathons were held in the US and Canada in 2019 with 498,665 finishers. Almost half a million people physically propelled their bodies for 26.2 miles. Not because it is fun or easy, but because they desire to accomplish something very challenging. Each runner endures the physically demanding and time-consuming training and preparation, keeping their vision in mind. It's hard, and it hurts, but I haven't come across anyone who said crossing the finish line wasn't worth it.

EMBRACING AND CONQUERING OBSTACLES

Like a marathon runner, you are going to have to endure the training and preparation needed to achieve your dream. You will likely encounter obstacles. Some will be in your control, and some won't. We often let fear become an obstacle that seems impossible to overcome. It shows up in many forms.

FEAR OF FAILURE

Opening the art gallery was a complete failure as a business, but as a learning experience, it was a victory. I tried something, I enjoyed it for a time, but it didn't work out. Annie F. Downs says this about failure: "If I would have never tried, I wouldn't have learned the power of failing at something. I just have to keep trying things that I'm not sure are going to work."[2]

There is always something to be gained when you fail. It doesn't mean that *you* are a failure; it means you need to take a closer look at what is working and what isn't. You might need to try something different or something entirely new. You might need a new location or further training.

Don't stop moving forward, and certainly don't return to something stagnant.

Michael Jordan and Babe Ruth are sports legends, known for being outstanding athletes. However, each had failures. At one point, Babe Ruth held the record for strikeouts and said, "Every strike brings me closer to the next home run."[3] Michael Jordan stated, "I've missed more than 9,000 shots in my career. I've lost almost 300 games. Twenty-six times, I've been trusted to take the game-winning shot and missed. I've failed over and over and over again in my life, and that is why I succeed."[4]

FEAR OF CRITICISM

When I started writing this book, it was fun. The words were spilling out of me, filling up pages. My fingers could barely keep up with my thoughts. It was thrilling to see a book beginning to emerge. At times, I was so energized I wanted to shout from the rooftops. Then, when it was time to start wrapping up, it became hard, really hard.

I was overwhelmed and filled with anxiety because I realized soon I would have to release these words into the hands of other eyes to critique, and then it would go out into the world where I had no more control. There were days when I thought I had made a mistake, days I thought it would be so much easier to go back to my old job, the place where no one leaves reviews about my work for the world to see. There is a quote from Elbert Hubbard that says, "There is only one way to avoid criticism: do nothing, say nothing, and be nothing."[5]

I was not being called to do nothing, say nothing, and be nothing. I had to keep pushing ahead to cross the finish line. Regardless of what the critics might say, I will have accomplished something I dreamed of doing.

FEAR OF REJECTION

There aren't many people who haven't heard of author J. K. Rowling and her *Harry Potter* books. It might not surprise you to know that J. K. Rowling was the first writer with a net worth of $1 billion. What might surprise you is her first *Harry Potter* book was passed up by twelve publishers before one accepted it. Sometimes rejection can lead you to a better place or make you work harder. Don't give up. Keep putting your work out there. Don't let setbacks and disappointment knock you off your path.

SLOW OR NO PROGRESS

Sometimes God will hold you to mold you or even change your mission. Don't be discouraged if the details of your dream shift. Be willing and open to change. It might be something small that is easily adjusted, or it might be something larger you didn't expect. This is a great time to go back to your expert or your social media group for advice. Don't be scared to ask for help. Don't be afraid to shift.

FLOODED WITH OPPORTUNITIES

Now, this might be an obstacle everyone desires! Sometimes, when you discover your calling and begin to follow your dream, you will get a flood of opportunities and ideas. When I was writing this book, I also wanted to work on a presentation, my website, and attend a conference. When I began jumping at every opportunity, I started to neglect one of the reasons I quit in the first place—family.

I was becoming a time hoarder and getting irritated when I had to sacrifice my writing time to do something for my family. I had to slow down, decide what was essential, and make it my primary focus. I also had to remember that part of my calling is to serve others, not myself. I had to say no and pass on some opportunities to be able to help my family and work on this book at the same time.

> Remember, your dream was given
> to you by God, and he is going
> to get you to the finish line.

When I remember this, I'm not so fearful, moving forward doesn't seem so scary, and the obstacles don't feel so big because I know God is leading me, and he is not going to lead me to the wrong place. Although, I might have to jump a few hurdles along the way.

CALL TO ACTION

Make a list of your obstacles.

Make a list of what you have tried. What is working and what is not?

What haven't you tried?

List all the things you are currently juggling and determine what is essential.

Prayer

Dear Lord,

Please give me the strength to overcome the obstacles that fall into my path and help me to remember my purpose. Guide me and provide me with clarity to see more of what you see. Allow me to change course when needed but continue to take steps toward the dream you have given me.

Amen.

Conclusion
LIVING THE DREAM

I can say that now I am living the dream I set out to accomplish. I am writing. It has not been easy sculpting a life that is so different from where I was before. Even though I don't have it all figured out and don't always get it right, when I sit down and write, my heart and soul come alive, and I feel filled with color.

In less than a year, I went from feeling empty, dreaming in my work office, to sitting at a desk in my home office writing the conclusion of this book. I dipped my toe in the waters of my dream, and as the waves of opportunity came rushing toward me, I finally left the shore and jumped in.

When I started out, I was focused on the process of writing and selling a book. I hoped I could help a few people and break even financially in the process.

I didn't count on learning so much about myself and realizing a calling is much more than what you do; it's about why you do it and who you do it for. It's a powerful, yet simple truth, not always easy to carry out and impossible to do alone. Luckily, I am not alone, and neither are you.

I dream that *you* will leave the shore and begin to chase your dream, even if you start by just dipping your toe in the water as I did. Begin with just one step, and then another, and then another, like when you get into a cold pool. At first, it's uncomfortable, but as you get used to it, it's pleasant, even delightful. Then you relax, focusing on the warm sun and enjoying the swim.

Now, I want to encourage you to stand up, put your feet on the floor, step out, and follow the path.

I encourage you to start now.

"May he give you the desire of your heart and make all your plans succeed" (Psalm 20:4).

Personality Inventory

Considering characteristics of your personality and having a list of skills, experiences, talents, and passions will help you navigate and gain clarity about what you want to do.

How do you describe yourself?

How do others describe you? (If you aren't sure, ask your friends, family, coworkers, and/or social media followers to list three words that describe you.)

What skills have you been taught or have developed over time?

What experiences have you lived through that might help you connect with others?

Do you have specific talent, something that you are naturally good at, for example, singing, athletics, listening, teaching, or creating?

What is your passion? What is that thing that you want to do that sets you on fire and makes you come alive?

About the Author

Lori Sanders is an author and speaker who grew up in South Texas and went to college in Central and West Texas. She holds a master's degree in communication disorders from Texas Tech University Health Sciences Center and worked as a speech-language pathologist for twenty-two years before following a dream to become a writer.

Now, Lori is working from home and writing as much as possible, her favorite topic being finding joy in simple living. She writes for her blog *Be Well, Heart and Soul* and has had her writing featured on the website nosidebar.com. Lori continues to be an active member of hope*writers and enjoys the camaraderie of her local mastermind group. Lori and her husband and son reside in East Texas.

CONNECT WITH LORI

LoriSanders.com
Facebook - @lorisandersauthor
Instagram - @lorisandersauthor

Endnotes

CHAPTER 1

1. Ken Ilgunas, *Walden on Wheels: On the Open Road from Debt to Freedom*, Kindle ed. (Boston: New Harvest, Houghton Mifflin Harcourt, 2013).

2. World Health Organization, "Burn-out an 'Occupational Phenomenon': International Classification of Diseases," accessed May 28, 2019, https://www.who.int/mental_health/evidence/burn-out/en/.

3. World Health Organization, "QD85 Burn-Out," *ICD-11* for Mortality and Morbidity Statistics, accessed April 2019, https://icd.who.int/browse11/l-m/en#/http://id.who.int/icd/entity/129180281.

4. "QD85 Burn-Out."

5. Ilgunas, *Walden on Wheels*.

6. Ilgunas, *Walden on Wheels*.

7. Tim Mannin, *Doing Things That Matter:*

Dream Wildly, Live Differently, Love Recklessly, Lead Courageously (Oklahoma City: Uptown Publishing, 2017).

CHAPTER 2

1. Sue Monk Kidd, Goodreads, accessed March 5, 2020, https://www.goodreads.com/work/quotes/25387072-the-invention-of-wings.

2. Paulo Coelho, *The Alchemist*, Kindle ed. (New York: HarperCollins Publishers, 2005).

3. Daniel Martínez Lara and Rafa Cano Mendez, dir. *Alike*. 2015, www.alike.es.

4. Emily P. Freeman, *The Next Right Thing*, "13: Quit Something," accessed March 23, 2020, https://emilypfreeman.com/podcast/the-next-right-thing/13/.

5. Freeman, "Quit Something."

6. Tom Rapsas, Wake Up Call, Patheos Explore the World's Faith through Different Perspectives on Religion and Spirituality! "Mother Teresa—On Why Loving Your Family Is the Most Important Thing You Can Do." last modified May 2, 2016, accessed February 2, 2020, www.patheos.com/blogs/wakeupcall/2016/05/advice-from-mother-

teresa-on-making-your-world-a-better-place/.

7. Unspoken, "Reason," *Reason*, 2014. iTunes app. Centricity Music.

CHAPTER 3

1. Jessica Honneger, *Imperfect Courage: Live a Life of Purpose by Leaving Comfort and Going Scared* (Colorado Springs: Water Brook, 2018).

2. Maria Goff, *Love Lives Here: Finding What You Need in a World Telling You What You Want* (Nashville: B&H Publishing Group, 2017).

3. Emily P. Freeman, *The Next Right Thing: A Simple, Soulful Practice for Making Life Decisions* (Ada, MI: Revell, 2019).

4. *Bird by Bird with Anne*, directed by Freida Lee Mock, performance by Anne Lamott, B001KL3H3A, Docudrama aired on March 31, 2009, on Amazon Prime, https://www.amazon.com/Bird-Anne-Lamott/dp/B003PN2OV2/ref=tmm_aiv_title_0?_encoding=UTF8&qid=&sr=.

CHAPTER 4

1. Leo F. Buscaglia, Goodreads, "A Quote by Leo F. Buscaglia," accessed March 3, 2020, www.goodreads.com/quotes/1200784-your-talent-is-god-s-gift-to-you-what-you-do.

2. Lassie Benton (pseudonym Elizabeth Appell), accessed March 3, 2020, https://www.goodreads.com/author/quotes/16483676.Lassie_Benton_pseudonym_of_Elizabeth_Appell_.

3. *Evan Almighty*, directed by Tom Shadyac, performance by Steve Carell, NBC Universal, aired in 2007, Amazon Prime, https://www.amazon.com/Evan-Almighty-Steve-Carell/dp/B000V69018.

4. Jennie Allen, *Restless: Because You Were Made for More*, Kindle ed. (Nashville: Thomas Nelson, 2013).

CHAPTER 5

1. Simon Sinek, AZ Quotes, accessed March 11, 2020, https://www.azquotes.com/quote/708455.

2. David Ramos, *What the Bible Says About Purpose*, Kindle ed. (Grand Rapids: Zondervan, 2017).

3. Pam Tebow, *Ripple Effects: Discover the Miraculous Motivation Power of a Woman's Influence* (Carol Stream, IL: Tyndale Momentum, 2019).

4. Michael Jr., "Know Your Why," last modified January 8, 2017, accessed January 16, 2020, https://www.youtube.com/watch?v=1ytFB8TrkTo.

5. Simon Sinek, "Simon Sinek," accessed January 16, 2020, simonsinek.com/.

6. Rachel Hollis, "Battling Burnout and Finding Your True Calling," RISE Podcast, 112, accessed January 31, 2020, https://thehollisco.com/blogs/podcasts/battling-burnout-finding-your-true-calling-with-ken-coleman.

CHAPTER 6

1. Peter Walsh, "Oprah Winfrey," accessed March 10, 2020, http://www.oprah.com/quote/peter-walsh-quote-clutter-isnt-just-the-stuff-in-your-closet..

2. Erika Oppenheimer, "Two Must Do's for Better Organization," Erika Oppenheimer, last modified June 3, 2014, accessed January 31, 2020,https://www.erikaoppenheimer.com/blog/two-organizational-must-dos.

3. Barbara Hemphill, accessed January 31, 2020, www.barbarahemphill.com.

CHAPTER 7

1. Bob Goff, *Love Does* (Nashville: Thomas Nelson, 2014).

2. Chris Anderson (CEO), "Ideas Worth Spreading," TED, accessed March 10, 2020, www.ted.com.

3. Richard K. Davis (President and CEO), Make-A-Wish America, accessed March 10, 2020, wish.org/

4. Kevin Johnson (President and CEO), Starbucks, accessed March 10, 2020, www.starbucks.com.

5. Rachel Hollis, "Battling Burnout and Finding Your True Calling," RISE Podcast, 112, accessed January 31, 2020, https://thehollisco.com/blogs/podcasts/battling-burnout-finding-your-true-calling-with-ken-coleman.

6. Annie F. Downs, "Brian Dixon," This Sounds Fun, 174, accessed October 8, 2019, https://www.anniefdowns.com/2019/10/08/episode-174-brian-dixon/.

CHAPTER 8

1. Nicholas Sparks, *Message in a Bottle*, eBook (New York: Grand Central Publishing, 1998).

2. Emily P. Freeman, host, "Writing for the Long Haul," hope*writers, 140, accessed March 23, 2020, https://podcasts.apple.com/us/podcast/40-writing-for-the-long-haul-with-annie-downs/id914574328?i=1000448401047.

3. Rachel Hodin, "35 Famous People Who Were Painfully Rejected Before Making it Big," Thought Catalog, last modified October 14, 2013, accessed January 31, 2020, https://thoughtcatalog.com/rachel-hodin/2013/10/35-famous-people-who-were-painfully-rejected-before-making-it-big/.

4. Scott Cole, "Michael Jordan 'Failure' Commercial HD 1080," Nike commercial, accessed January 31, 2020, www.youtube.com/watch?v=JA7G7AV-LT8.

5. Elbert Hubbard, Goodreads, accessed March 10, 2020, https://www.goodreads.com/work/quotes/9142221-little-journeys-to-the-homes-of-the-great-vol-3-american-statesmen.

Made in the USA
Coppell, TX
15 May 2020